Commissioned by and dedicated to
Grex Vocalis
and its leader
Carl Høgset

Arne Nordheim

TRES LAMENTATIONES

Secundum Hieremiam Prophetam

Edition Wilhelm Hansen A/S, Copenhagen

I
Quomodo sedit sola civitas plena
popolu
facta est quasi vidua domina
gentium
princeps provinciarum facta est
sub tributo
                          Lam. 1 (1)

II
Clamavit cor eorum ad Dominum
super muros filiae Sion
Deduc quasi torrentem lacrimas
per diem et per noctem
                          Lam. 2 (18–)

III
Converte nos Domine ad te et
convertemur innova dies nostros
sicut a principio
sed proiciens reppulisti nos iratus
es contra nos vehementer
                          Lam. 5 (21 & 22)

How doth the city sit solitary, that
    was full of people!
How is she become as a widow!
She that was great among the nations, and
    princess among the provinces,
How is she become tributary!

Their heart cried unto the Lord,
O wall of the daughter of Zion,
    let tears run down like
    river day and night.

Turn thou us unto thee, O Lord, and we
    shall be turned;
Renew our days as of old.
But thou hast utterly rejected us;
Thou art very wroth against us.

TRES LAMENTATIONES

Secundum Hieremiam Prophetam

I

Arne Nordheim, 1985

B

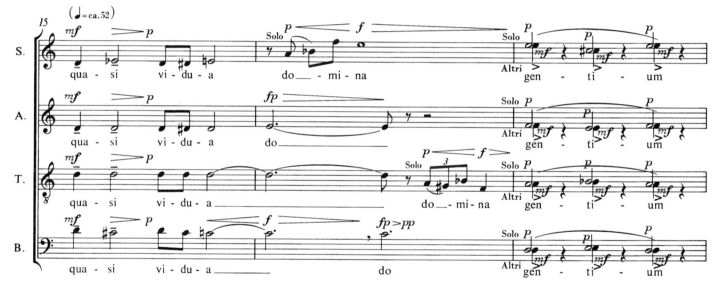

II

III